Lollipops
and
Parachutes

Lollipops
and
Parachutes

120 Stimulating Learning Activities
for Children of Active,
Caring Adults

DONNA STISCAK

McGRAW-HILL BOOK COMPANY

New York   St. Louis   San Francisco
Toronto   Hamburg   Mexico

1 2 3 4 5 6 7 8 9 F G R F G R 8 7 6 5 4

ISBN 0-07-061503-9

LIBRARY OF CONGRESS CATALOGING IN PUBLICATION DATA
Stiscak, Donna.
   Lollipops and parachutes.
      1. Educational games.   2. Creative activities and seat
work.   3. Creative thinking.   I. Title.
GV1480.S75   1984   649'.51   83-26755
ISBN 0-07-061503-9

Book design by Roberta Rezk

69192

This book is dedicated to
Melissa,
who was the first lollipop.

ACKNOWLEDGMENTS

Linda J. Wilyot   M.S.W., Social Research, Administration, and Planning, University of Pittsburgh

Ellen L. Woods   B.S., Speech Pathology, Carlow College

Margaret L. Woods Ph.D., Counselor Education, University of Pittsburgh

CONTENTS

PREFACE

Activities in *Lollipops and Parachutes* are grouped by age; in each category, the activity is matched to the child's learning needs at that particular age. Age categories can serve as a guideline in selecting beginning activities.

For a child to complete these activities successfully, other factors, in addition to age, are important. Some children acquire skills that are consistent with their development at a younger or older age than is "expected." Maturity also influences the child's ability to concentrate on an activity and gain insight from it.

Children who are ready to learn may need to practice this type of critical/creative thinking process. For familiarity and review, begin these children with activities in a lower age category. On the other hand, some of the activities designed for older children can be opportunities for younger children to practice new skills or develop existing ones.

Many of the activities in *Lollipops and Parachutes* can be adjusted to allow for differences among children in growth and development. The intent of the age categories is not to be limiting, but rather to suggest a general range of ability and interest.

INTRODUCTION

Lollipops and Parachutes is a book of rewards and freedom. The best reward in the world (lollipops) is the feeling of self-worth and competence that comes with success in life. The aim of this book is to help children develop sharp skills, to learn to think creatively, and to have fun while doing so.

Lollipops and Parachutes is a book of rewards and freedom. Adults can stay balanced, and, like the parachutist, move freely within their own lives while guiding their children effectively. The activities in this book are designed so that adults have enough time and energy for their other pleasures and responsibilities.

Lollipops and Parachutes is a book for busy people who care deeply about their child's development. Some of these people wish they had more time to spend with their children to stimulate their mental growth. Others wonder how they can provide enrichment opportunities when time is available. Since every situation can be an occasion for learning, you can *start today to teach your child to think!*

Lollipops and Parachutes is a book for people who want to use their time and energy astutely, without spending money, while helping their children develop creative and critical thinking skills.

As a classroom educator and elementary and secondary school counselor, I have been involved with children's development and the role that parents can effectively play in this development. Having worked with students from Kindergarten through grade 12, and talked to hundreds of parents, I am convinced that there is a definite need for the integration of school and home learning experiences.

To the trained professional, differences in learning ability become apparent as early as Kindergarten. Often, the ability of some children to progress faster in school is due to early opportunities and enrichments! Therefore, whether critical thinking takes place in a classroom or living room, the learning benefits are the same.

What is critical thinking? Some people assume that if you can remember a lot of facts and study hard, then you are learning. Yes, you may be learning to memorize, concentrate, or play back information. But information that is not reasoned out, analyzed, and applied has little value.

Critical thinking happens when a child looks at an object and begins to explore how that object is similar to or different from other objects. When a child can see a pattern with designs or numbers, or can imagine a plant talking or create a flower from a necklace, then that child is thinking creatively, as well as critically.

My interest in critical thinking has led me to take the basics of learning theory and apply them to games and activities you can use almost any time—especially your busiest times. These activities are designed for parents, grandparents, babysitters, and friends who want to satisfy the needs of other children as well as their own.

The activities presented in this book have several unique features:

1. You do not need to buy more games and toys. You need only basic materials that are usually found in most homes with young children.
2. You do not need special artistic talent or mechanical skill. Activities and projects are simple to plan and carry out.
3. For the most part, the activities can be self-directed by

the child. With practice, he or she can do most of these activities independently.

4. You will not need more time in your 26-hour day! You can be doing other things at the same time as you direct or participate with your child in these activities.

Home learning experiences are valuable for another reason. *You* create the learning environment and conditions. At no other time in a child's life will you have the full power to vary the setting, time period, materials, and rewards as in those precious early years. Have your child develop critical thinking abilities in the most supportive environment . . . by utilizing the most supportive person—*you.*

The activities in *Lollipops and Parachutes* are designed and categorized to meet the developmental needs of children. The activities have been placed in the age group that most developmental experts view as appropriate. For some children, these learning activities are used more effectively at a younger or older age.

Educators have designated certain skills as crucial to a child's successful performance in school. Reading and reasoning skills are the primary skills required for school success. Children should begin to develop these skills before they begin school. The amazing part of this learning process is that just with experience and maturation, the child masters many skills without formal instruction. Just imagine—you can enhance and sharpen these abilities by interacting with the child's natural curiosity about new and challenging experiences. What a difference this can make when the child enters the competitive world!

Lollipops and Parachutes contains a Reasoning Skills Supplement designed to help meet the need to develop school skills. This supplement consists of activities aimed at developing numerical reasoning, sequential reasoning, and analysis skills.

An Educational Reference Guide is provided in the back of the book. The guide identifies for you the primary skills that are developed in each activity.

Keep in mind that each of these activities is more effective when followed by some kind of reward. Rewarding a child for a successful attempt at a task is vital! Children, like adults, seek "pay-offs" for their actions, and all positive behaviors need to be reinforced with immediate and well-defined rewards.

Remember: Rewards can take many forms. Your compliments, smiles of approval, and hugs and kisses are readily available and highly effective rewards. Some special treats and privileges (even a lollipop) can be given from time to time.

I suggest that you first read all the activities described in this book and then select those that are most appropriate for your young one. The activities and objects included are suggested as examples that may require some modification and discretion if your child has exceptional needs. Use your critical thinking skills and imagination to adapt any activity to a higher or lower level.

Allow *Lollipops and Parachutes* to lighten your burdens . . . so your real cares can grow! Experience the satisfaction of being up and above each and every situation.

And enjoy that lollipop!

1

TALKATIVE WAYS ~
TRANQUIL DAYS
Activities for Children
Aged 3 to 4

Where the Little People Live

HERE'S HOW:

Children can use their toys and household items to build a make-believe city or mall. Building kits can be used to create houses, stores, a fire station, a school, an ice-skating rink, an ice-cream stand, and a movie theater. Artificial flowers can indicate a garden or park. A self-constructed paper cone can be used as the roof for an ice-cream stand. Pictures cut from magazines can identify various types of stores. An airport can be shown by using a favorite airplane or helicopter. Make a train station or motorcycle shop. Remember to line your streets with those little toy people . . . and put those animals in a zoo.

1

HERE'S WHAT ELSE: Those little people and animals can march through the
town on a parade day. Celebrate
special holidays by decorating
the town with an appropriate
theme. Play music for an added
effect.

Now You See It, Now You Don't

HERE'S HOW:

Place familiar objects, such as a toy, salt and pepper shakers, a piece of fruit, a napkin, a spoon, etc., on a table. Begin this activity with two objects. Have the child touch and name each object. Be sure that you identify each object by name several times. Some children will want to repeat the names of these objects aloud with you. Next, send the child out of the room and remove the objects from the table. Call the child back, and ask him to place them where they were before.

Increase the number of objects on the table as the child replaces them correctly.

HERE'S WHAT ELSE:

Select four familiar objects that differ in function and place them on a flat surface, specifically limiting the area to two square feet. Again, name and touch each object several times. This time, when the child leaves the room, remove one object. When he returns, ask him which object is missing. Then have him place that object back in its original location. Change objects and follow the same procedure. This time, however, add an object while the child is out of the room. When he returns, have him name or point to the new object.

Make this activity a game by switching roles with the child.

Stroke the Memory

HERE'S HOW:
Find photographs and mementos of the child, family, and friends doing different things, for example, at birthday parties, or on holidays and vacations. Referring to these items, recall with the child as many details of the experience as possible. Always relate the experience to the present. For example, after looking at pictures or a gift from a second birthday party, say, "This year you are going to have a third birthday party." Then take the experience into the future by saying, "Last year we had a picture of a dog on the cake. What kind of cake do you want this year?"

HERE'S WHAT ELSE: Find pictures showing the
child doing activities during dif-
ferent seasons of the year.
Speak to the child or have the
child speak to you about the
differences in activities, clothing,
and weather from one season to
the next. For example, ask the
child, "What are you wearing in
this picture (of the child in
swimsuit)?" and "Where would
you go wearing your swimsuit?"
Or, if the picture is of the child
in a snowsuit, you might ask,
"What did you do when you
wore this outfit?" or "What do
you have on your hands?"

I See It First

HERE'S HOW: Play the game "I see it first" by having the child look for objects while traveling in a car or a train. You could say, for example, "Let's see who will be the first one to see a . . ." and finish with a gas station, a cow, a white car, or a stop sign, whatever is appropriate. Select the object most likely to be viewed while traveling the next few minutes or mile.

HERE'S WHAT ELSE: Adapt this activity to the home by selecting an area of the house and activities that take place in that area. "Who will be the first to see the toast popping (the coffee percolating, and the timer ready to sound)?"

Nonsensical Conversation

HERE'S HOW: Begin a sentence, but finish
                             it with a silly, nonsense ending.
                             For example, "A man came into
                             a restaurant and ordered camel
                             soup and a pigburger." Encour-
                             age the child to make up crea-
                             tive sentences.

HERE'S WHAT ELSE: Have the child pretend that
                             the names of foods can be
                             changed. Ask the child to think
                             of new names for foods that are
                             familiar to him. A few starters
                             you might suggest are white
                             shells (eggs), half-moon (ba-
                             nana), and sweet-stick (lollipop).

Picture It with Words

HERE'S HOW:

Sitting with the child, look at a picture and begin to describe it. Encourage the child to think about the information presented in the picture by asking questions such as "Is this a picture of winter or summer?"

"How can you tell?"

"Is the little boy happy or sad?"

"What do you think happened to make him feel that way?"

Encourage the child to make up a story about the situation in the picture by asking "What happened before?"

"What will come next?"

"How will it end?"

HERE'S WHAT ELSE: Set out photographs of
family members, friends, and
pictures of cartoon characters.
Think of a familiar expression or
mannerism that one of the people pictured uses frequently. Say
that expression or describe the
mannerism and have the child
guess which person (picture)
you are referring to.

For example, ask the child
"Who always says, 'Hi there—
punky do'?" Have the child pick
up the correct picture. Switch
roles after all the pictures have
been removed.

What Would Happen If . . .

HERE'S HOW:

Play the imagination game "What would happen if . . ." by completing an imaginary thought with some sensible comment. For instance, "If the curtains could talk, what would they say?"

Some other possibilities are the following:

"If the chairs could walk, where would they go?"

"If the ceiling dropped ten feet, what would it hit?"

"If the plants could sing, what song would they choose?"

"If the windows could see, what would they be looking at?"

HERE'S WHAT ELSE: Develop a child's imagination by having the child pretend
that he is something else. Suggest that the child pretend to be
a tree, the wind, a car, or a cat.
Ask the child for additional roles
to play. Place the names of
these roles in a hat (or bag) so
that each person gets to select
a role to play. Take turns acting
out the selected roles and try to
guess the other's role.

Bathe a Boat

HERE'S HOW:

(This is an outdoor activity, or one for a room such as the bathroom or kitchen that you don't mind getting soapy and wet from end to end.)

Fill a bucket or basin with soapy water or bubble bath. Get a discarded toothbrush, a dry cloth, and fill a window-cleaner spray bottle with water. With the toothbrush and soapy water, have the child scrub each toy clean; then, spray-rinse them until no soap is visible. Dry with cloth.

HERE'S WHAT ELSE:

If you have an extra lettuce spinner, have the child put small toys in it and "spin" them dry. The spinner may not dry very well, but it does fascinate young children.

Taste Test

HERE'S HOW: Select and prepare several
samples of food, each having a
distinct taste and texture. Tell
the child that you want him to
conduct a "taste test," and tell
him that all the foods are things
he likes. Have the child close his
eyes and taste one of the samples and identify what he has
sampled. Recommended food
items are applesauce, peanut
butter, and whipped cream.

HERE'S WHAT ELSE: Following the same procedure, conduct a "touch test."
Place a small sample of applesauce, peanut butter, and
whipped cream on three plates.
Let the child feel the texture and
consistency of each substance.
With eyes closed, have him
identify each sample by touch.

Change the Chain

HERE'S HOW: Give your child a discarded
costume jewelry necklace (the
longer and stronger the better).
String or yarn can be used in
place of a necklace. Demonstrate how the chain can be
made into different shapes and
designs. For example, shape the
chain into a circle; change the
circle to form a square. Make
the chain look like a worm or
snake, a lollipop or tree.

HERE'S WHAT ELSE: Use household props to
add more features. For exam-
ple, the chain could become a
flower, and a straw become the
stem. The chain could be
shaped to resemble a car and
lids of jars be used as wheels.
Experiment with different materials, such as pipe-cleaners, bottle caps, and parts of toys.

Once Upon a Time

HERE'S HOW:

The next time you tell a story, make one up by having everyone participate. Begin by saying, "Once upon a time, there was a girl. . . ." Have each person contribute one phrase or idea to the story. After a few minutes the story invariably becomes unique and draws in even people who are most often listeners.

HERE'S WHAT ELSE:

Use this activity to recall the past, discuss the present, and create the future. Some good starting lines are:

1. Once upon a time, when I was a baby. . . .
2. Today I am. . . .
3. When I get big I will. . . .

Tour Guide

HERE'S HOW:

Have a tape recorder on hand during a road trip, or improvise by using a hand microphone made out of rolled paper. Have the child pretend to be a tour guide and describe the sights and scenes along the way. To help the child increase his vocabulary, ask him to try to use different words to describe the same objects. For example, a road could be called a thruway, highway, turnpike, parkway, bypass, street, avenue, or Route 66.

HERE'S WHAT ELSE:

Make a "talk show" by having the child interview other people on a specific topic. You may need to demonstrate this activity by interviewing the child first. Another way to get this activity started is to allow the child to role-play his favorite television character. You can create added pleasure from this experience by playing back the interview.

Follow the Leader

HERE'S HOW:

Sit facing the child and begin to make a pattern of bodily motions. For example, touch your elbow, thumb, chin, ear, and knee. Have the child imitate you by touching the same parts of his body, in exactly the same order. Start with two or three motions, and work up to as many as the child can imitate successfully. All motions are to be followed without any verbal instructions. Reverse roles. After the child understands the game, have the child practice on a favorite toy, such as a doll or stuffed animal.

HERE'S WHAT ELSE:

Following the same format as above, demonstrate bodily expressions that show different moods, such as happiness or sadness. Create some humorous effects by standing in front of a mirror.

Point and Find

HERE'S HOW: Hide an object in a room.
Using nonverbal instructions,
guide the child in searching for
the object. Point left, right, forward; motion to proceed, stop,
turn around, bend over, stand
on tiptoes; nod yes or no; and
use hands and fingers to indicate steps and show distance.
Reverse roles so the child can
practice using nonverbal com-
munication.

HERE'S WHAT ELSE: A variation of this game is
to allow the child to look for the
hidden object by exploring the
room as he wishes. This time,
only give clues to let the child
know he is near the hidden object. Suggested words would be
burning-up, hot, warm, luke-
warm, cold, and freezing.

Classifying Clutter

HERE'S HOW:

Save all junk mail and store it in an empty shoe box. When it comes time to clean, give the child the job of "filing" all the junk mail. To do this, have a very simple and efficient filing system, such as color-coding five shoe boxes and color-coding each piece of mail with Magic Marker or crayon on the envelope. The child must open the envelope, take out the letter, put the same color mark on the letter as on the envelope, and store it in the same-colored box.

HERE'S WHAT ELSE:

Advertisements with pictures on them can be sorted as to who would be most likely to enjoy having that object. Boxes can then be labeled, "Mom, Dad, Grandma, me."

No Speeding

HERE'S HOW:
Designate an area approximately two feet by eight feet and collect an assortment of toys and household items. With a little imagination, a child can use these articles to construct tunnels, lakes, bridges, and mountains. Instruct the child to arrange the toys so as to create "obstacles" that will make passage more difficult. Using his favorite car or train, he can then steer the vehicle through the obstacle course. Have him increase his speed as his skill improves. You might find arrows helpful in charting the direction.

HERE'S WHAT ELSE:
Build another roadway using a deck of playing cards or set of dominoes. This time, instead of avoiding the objects, the child is to follow the roadway walking only on the cards or dominoes.

The Times when You're in Lines

HERE'S HOW:

Take the child grocery shopping with you and use a handwritten or picture list to check the items in the shopping cart before going to the check-out line. For a younger child, read the list one item at a time and have the child point to or touch the correct item. Gradually increase the number of items you say before having the child identify them. For example, you might say, "Point to the bread, butter, milk, and sugar."

HERE'S WHAT ELSE:

Use all situations in which you have to wait as learning experiences. For example, in the pediatrician's office, have the child count the number of other children in the room, and ask "How many children came in before you did, and how many came after?"

The Beginning, Middle, and End

HERE'S HOW: Draw a waving line from left
to right across the width of a
piece of paper. Trace the design
onto another sheet of paper.
Cut one sheet of paper vertically
into three strips so that the line
is broken in three places. Rearrange the strips of paper. Have
the child put the cut pieces together so they match the duplicate. If the child completes the
task successfully, the line will be
uninterrupted from beginning to
end. For older children, use
headlines in the newspaper or
comic strips.

HERE'S WHAT ELSE: This exercise can be used
to develop the child's ability to
act out a visual process. Walk
an imaginary waving line, then
have the child duplicate your
exact movements.

2

CHANGING PACE~
TIME FOR SPACE
Activities for Children
Aged 5 to 6

Carving a Clean Face

HERE'S HOW:

Store small bars of soap in a plastic container. If you are working with a young child, use a nontoxic Magic Marker; with an older child, an emery board or pen can be used. Before beginning the exercise, place the soap in water to soften it. Then have the child create a face on each bar of soap. He can entertain himself repeatedly by carving a face, then rinsing it off and saving the soap for future use.

HERE'S WHAT ELSE:

Many materials can be added to the soap bar for effect. Cotton balls can be used for a beard, scraps of yarn for hair, and cotton swabs or toothpicks for arms and legs. Soap can also be cut into smaller pieces for building material.

Designer Original

HERE'S HOW:

(This is an activity for a youngster with above-average manual dexterity.)

Give the child a box of buttons with large holes. This activity also requires a needle; the type of needle you will want to use will vary depending on the child's age. Very young children can use a shoestring; older children, a needlepoint needle. If a shoestring is used, then thread is not needed. With a shoestring the child can sew (shoestring) the buttons together or tape them onto paper to form a design. If a needlepoint needle is used, the child can create "a designer original" with remnant material and yarn. An older child can sew individual buttons on the fabric to complete a design.

HERE'S WHAT ELSE:

For all young children, a design can be drawn on any remnant material. You can use chalk, pencil, or Magic Marker. Then, the child can sew the buttons on the outline or use the buttons as accents (door knobs, chimneys, wheels).

Making a List, Checking It Twice

HERE'S HOW:

In order to complete this activity, separate and save the following items from food product packaging: box tops, package wraps, coupons, and advertisements. Arrange the items by food groups so that the child can see the groups that are available. Have the child help make a shopping list by selecting a desirable number of items from each food group. The child can then paste on paper all selected items to use for a shopping list. Before you unpack your groceries, give the child the pasted list. As you unpack each item on the list, show the child the item and have him cross off the matching product identification.

HERE'S WHAT ELSE:

Shopping lists can be made for other purchases as well, such as clothes, toys, cleaning materials, and activities. Save catalogs and magazines for ideas to select for future use.

Stroll around the Roll

HERE'S HOW:

Save empty paper towel rolls (safe and cheap). When you have at least six rolls, you can design a very simple exercise to improve coordination. Designate an area about 18 inches wide and 7 feet long to be used for this activity. Set the rolls on end about one foot apart from each other in a straight row. Have the child walk around the rolls, weaving in and out, without going outside the marked area. The object is to control body movements so as not to knock down any of the rolls.

HERE'S WHAT ELSE:

Using the same setup, have the child hop, walk backwards, or do a heel-to-toe walk around the rolls. Older children can time themselves and record the amount of time needed to complete the activity.

No Jokers Here!

HERE'S HOW:

A deck of cards can entertain children for hours and, if used creatively, can teach many important skills. A good game is to select four cards, one from each suit. Describe the differences in the suits using words the child is likely to remember. (For example, hearts can be associated with "I love you," or "Valentine's Day.") Then, with the remaining deck in your hand, turn up one card at a time and let the child match the card with one of the four suits already chosen.

HERE'S WHAT ELSE:

One variation of this game is to use the numbers on the cards instead of the suits, and have the child select cards numbered 2 through 10 and place them in numerical order.

Card Castles

HERE'S HOW: Use a deck of playing cards
to build houses, garages, tun-
nels, tents, and castles. Stand
two cards upright so that they
lean against each other. The
cards should touch at the top to
form a triangle with the floor as
the base. The cards can also be
placed at a 90-degree angle,
leaning against each other.
Roofs can be added by placing
cards gently on the top of four
leaning cards arranged in a
square. Hint: Begin by leaning
the cards against a wall or base-
board. This creates a sturdier
structure and support for the
very young child.

HERE'S WHAT ELSE: Choose some small toys,
such as cars, or doll house fur-
niture, and place these objects
on a flat surface. Have the child
build a garage or a house
by placing cards around
the objects.

Future Physician

HERE'S HOW:
Make a simple sketch of the outline of the human body. Name the parts of the body, and have the child indicate, by drawing or coloring, the parts of the body as you name them. It is a good idea to select those parts of the body that a doctor is most likely to examine, and to do this activity before a visit to the doctor's office to add some humor and to reduce tension.

HERE'S WHAT ELSE:
After the visit to the doctor, have the child circle on his drawing all the body parts examined by the doctor. Have the child circle with a different color marker the parts of the body the doctor examined that were not indicated in the original drawing.

Forget It Not

HERE'S HOW:

Look at a picture in a magazine with your child, pointing out specific colors, shapes, and objects. Then, allow the child to study the picture for a few minutes. Close the magazine and ask your child questions about what you looked at together. By closing the magazine, you are less likely to ask for information that is too specific—this will sharpen your memory, too!

HERE'S WHAT ELSE:

In addition to studying the objects in the picture, have the child examine the people (ages, sex, clothing, expressions), and the actions (walking, swimming, eating) they are engaged in.

Guess What Is in My Purse

HERE'S HOW:

To play the game "Guess what is in my purse," begin with the sentence, "I have something in my purse that will spill." Give clues to stimulate the child to think of logical answers. For example, you may want the child to say, "nail polish." You may need to give other clues, such as "It's red and in a glass bottle."

HERE'S WHAT ELSE:

Select an object from your purse or elsewhere and ask the child to name as many different uses for it as he can think of. For example, nail polish can be used to polish the nails, to stop a run in panty hose, and as an identifying mark on items. Expand this activity to include other articles, such as Band-Aids, masking tape, and emery boards.

I'm Thinking about Something

HERE'S HOW:

Play the favorite children's game, "I'm thinking about something. . . ." Use phrases that lead the child to guess what you are thinking about that is in the room at the time. For example, "I'm thinking about something that is round like a ball. I'm thinking about something that is very soft."

HERE'S WHAT ELSE:

To change the activity, give a clue that describes what the object is not. For example, "I'm thinking about something that will *not* break if I drop it."

Tally the Taffy

HERE'S HOW:

Have the child add up the items that are being placed in a shopping cart, being unpacked at home, or are accessible for counting. Give the child paper and pencil to tally the products, using numbers or slash marks. (Decide whether six apples in a bag is one item or six items.) There are many ways a child can keep an accurate count of the items. To keep a total, the child can use a game board with a peg and holes, pennies in a change purse, or pieces of old yarn tied around the legs of a table or a shopping cart (be sure to remove yarn before leaving the store).

HERE'S WHAT ELSE:

Before going shopping, have the child take an inventory of items regularly used by the family. For example, you might instruct the child to "count all the bars of soap, rolls of towels, and cans of soup."

I See Something

HERE'S HOW: Take turns naming objects
in view, beginning with all
sounds of the alphabet that are
familiar to the child. An example
is, "I see something that begins
with the sound 'b.'"

HERE'S WHAT ELSE: Change the activity by using rhyming words. For exam-
ple, "I see something that
sounds like 'tall.'" Use colors or
shapes, such as something red
or round.

Scavenger Hunt

HERE'S HOW:

While driving in heavy city traffic, suggest to the child that he count the number of restaurants, gas stations, drugstores, or empty parking spaces along the way. Set a reasonable length of time or distance. A few city blocks or five minutes should be the limit of attention for this exercise.

HERE'S WHAT ELSE:

Rather than looking for the same kind of business establishment, name three or four different kinds of businesses and have the child find one of each kind. For example, you might say, "See if you can find a restaurant, gas station, drugstore, and a bank before the next traffic light."

The Butcher, the Baker,
the "Candystick" Maker

HERE'S HOW:

Take with you on a trip to a shopping center something to use for counting different types of stores. Items such as jelly beans, pennies, or stickers can be used. Select a specific kind of store for the child to recognize, such as all stores that sell shoes. Each time you pass this kind of store, the child is to put a jelly bean in an envelope. At the end of the shopping trip the jelly beans can be "cashed in" for some prize or be a treat by themselves. Increase the difficulty by adding conditions, such as shoe stores on the left side, or men's clothes stores on the right side.

HERE'S WHAT ELSE: After the child has prac-
ticed the above activity, have
him repeat it. Ask the child to
identify stores that sell specific
products or services to meet
human needs. For example,
"Spot needs dog food; where do
we get it?" "Baby needs diapers;
where do we buy them?" "My
shoes need to be fixed; where
do I take them?"

Magazine Jigsaw Puzzle

HERE'S HOW: Select an interesting picture
in a magazine or old book. Let
your child paste the picture on a
piece of cardboard or construction paper that is the same size
as the picture. Then cut this
mounted picture into small, irregular pieces. Scramble the
pieces. The child must put the
pieces together to make the
picture. For older children,
make a jigsaw puzzle out of a
large number, letter, or word
printed on paper. Paste on cardboard, cut up, and have the
child put it together.

HERE'S WHAT ELSE: Have the child draw a picture and cut it up. Put it back
together.

Making Fluffy Animals

HERE'S HOW:

Save discarded bars of soap, empty toilet tissue rolls, hair spray can tops, spools of thread, or small plastic spoons. Give the child a squeeze bottle of glue and cotton balls and have him create an animal from the object by covering it with the cotton balls. Perhaps a favorite book of animal pictures will help to stimulate the imagination.

HERE'S WHAT ELSE:

Create features for the animals by using household items and children's favorites, such as raisins or Cheerios for eyes, Shredded Wheat for eyebrows and beard, broom bristles for whiskers, buttons for eyes or nose, peanuts for teeth, and popsicle sticks for legs.

Clean the Cabin

HERE'S HOW:

Together with your child, group into three categories all items to be arranged or put away in the bedroom. Categories could be toys and games, books, clothing, and shoes. Then have the child make label cards with each of the categories printed or pictured on the cards, one category on each card. Make about five sets of cards.

Straightening up the room can become a game if you take the cards and place the appropriate card on each item that is out of place. The next time, the child will be able to do this himself. When the child puts his toys away, or hangs up his clothing, he then places the card into a "happy-face" box. A shoe box or envelope can be decorated as the happy-face card container. After all the chores are completed, cards can be counted and special treats given as rewards.

HERE'S WHAT ELSE: Teach the child to place
dirty clothes in the proper ham-
per or basket by decorating this
container with a "frowning
face." Every time an article of
clothing is placed in the "frowning face," the child gets a
"happy-face" card in return.

Follow That Tune

HERE'S HOW: Record on tape, or buy a
commercial recording of the
child's favorite song, nursery
rhyme, or jingle. After the child
learns the words, play the song
while your child sings along.
Then play the song again, and
while the song is playing, turn
down or shut off the volume for
about five seconds and then
turn it up/on again. Continue to
do this throughout the recording. This will create a gap for
the child to fill in with the correct words. The object is for the
child to practice timing
and learn to be in sync with
the recording.

HERE'S WHAT ELSE: Using another song, assign
certain words as "cues" for the
child to respond to by hopping.
For example, you might say,
"Every time you hear the word
'farmer,' hop one time." Other
responses might be clapping,
jumping, and turning around.

A Place for Everything

HERE'S HOW: Place on a table all the items needed for a meal, that is, silverware, napkins, plates, glasses. Have the child use these items to create a place setting by following your instructions. Give simple instructions, such as "Put the spoon to the left of the knife," or "Place the fork on the napkin."

HERE'S WHAT ELSE: Once the child is able to follow simple instructions, you can expand them by using more complex terms, such as to the right of, to the left of, next to, above, below, on top of, underneath, at the bottom of, at the top of, opposite, between, within, in a row, and diagonally.

The Aim Is the Game

HERE'S HOW: Gather containers that have
a fairly wide opening, such as
coffee cans or milk containers.
Place these containers in a row.
Give the child several pennies or
any object that can be thrown
safely. Have the child stand
erect next to the containers.
Begin by having the child drop
the objects, one at a time, into
the containers, moving from left
to right. If space permits, instruct the child to move back
one foot each time he gets all
the objects in the containers.

HERE'S WHAT ELSE: Vary the size of the openings of the containers. Use a
reward system to encourage the
child to try for the containers
with smaller openings. One container can be designated as the
"jackpot"; others could yield
stickers, treats, etc.

Sewing Friends

HERE'S HOW:

Empty spools of thread can be turned into characters or little "sewing friends." Give the child crayons or markers and have him draw and color a face on one side of the spool. Scraps of thread, yarn, and material can be used to add hair, hats, and mustaches. To make the body, connect a straw through the hole of the spool. Place one end of the straw in a flat eraser, sponge, or sand pile so that it stands upright. Using glue or tape, attach smaller pieces of straw for the arms and legs.

HERE'S WHAT ELSE:

Consider setting up a play with the little "sewing friends." Give the characters names, occupations, and personalities.

Color Me Clean

HERE'S HOW: When laundry time comes,
let the child be a helper with
tasks he is likely to be able to
handle. Sorting laundry, for instance, can be his chore. Depending on your individual
washing style, sorting can be
done by color, by category (all
towels), or by wear (all play
clothes).

HERE'S WHAT ELSE: Remember to have the little
helper around when it comes
time to match socks, fold
clothes, and put clothes away.

Guess Who's Coming to Dinner

HERE'S HOW: When you are expecting company, make a game out of guessing the guest list and preparing name place cards for everyone. Begin by giving the child verbal clues as to who the guests are. For instance, you might ask, "What man gave you a shirt for your birthday?" After the guests have been identified, have the child make name place cards. This can be done by using three-by-five-inch note cards. Demonstrate how to fold the note card in half horizontally so it will stand. Older children can print names on the cards; younger children can decorate. Show child where to place each card.

HERE'S WHAT ELSE: Color-code the name cards by placing a dot of color on the inside and have a door prize! How about making favors for everyone, too?

Category Game

HERE'S HOW: Start the game by naming
a category. Select a pattern of
hand motions or beat for all to
follow in naming items from
that category. For example, the
rhythm can be two hand claps,
name an item; or two lap slaps,
name an item. Take turns naming one item each in keeping
with the beat. Some good categories are colors, fruits, vegeta-
bles, animals, insects, books,
holidays, musical instruments,
and occupations. As the child's
skill increases, use categories
describing action, such as summer activities, preparations for a
holiday, or weather conditions.

HERE'S WHAT ELSE: Play the game by having
each person name items from a
category he has chosen secretly.
See who can be the first person
to guess the other's category.

Throwing-Go-Round

HERE'S HOW:

Place four empty containers, boxes, or buckets around the child. One container should be placed in front and one in back of the child; one to the left and one to the right of the child. Each should be about a foot away from him. Instruct the child to stand still and, moving only his arms, drop preselected objects into a container in a clockwise fashion.

HERE'S WHAT ELSE:

Distinguish containers by color, shape, size, or picture and designate the container that is the target. Alternate sequence and increase speed gradually.

Thread Painting

HERE'S HOW:

Strips of thread and yarn pasted on construction paper or cardboard can be used to create a picture or design. Place the thread on the paper and have the child shape the thread to create an object (flower), a design (circle, square), or a picture (rainbow, seashore). Glue each piece of thread as it is shaped. A finished product could include blue threads for ocean waves, beige threads for sand, and a yellow sun.

HERE'S WHAT ELSE:

To turn these original designs into greeting cards for special occasions, help the child write appropriate messages.

Your License, Please

HERE'S HOW: While driving, have your child look at license plates and identify letters or numbers in sequence. Look for the letters A through Z, or the numbers 1 through 10 in sequence. Let the child use any group of letters or numbers on a given plate, as long as they flow from left to right. For example, a license plate with the sequence AFB172 could be used for letters A and B, and for numbers 1 and 2.

HERE'S WHAT ELSE: Make this game a little more challenging by adding some ground rules. For example, make it a rule that the car must be in front, or moving and not parked, or that only red, white, or blue cars count.

Memory Fun

HERE'S HOW:

Start the game by saying, "I'm going on a picnic, and I'm bringing a basket." Ask the child to repeat the same sentence and add something else to take along. He may say, "I'm going on a picnic, and I'm bringing a basket and a ball." Take turns, adding one item each time. Change the sentence to any activity the child can relate to. For example, "I'm going swimming and I'm bringing a bathing suit."

HERE'S WHAT ELSE:

Alter the game by adding a rule, such as that all things named must begin with the "D" sound or any sound that you know is familiar to the child. Or, select items that can be categorized, such as all red items.

Hide and Find

HERE'S HOW:

Hide an object in a room. Give the child only verbal instructions on how to find the object. Make the instructions specific and simple. Introduce new directional terms, such as opposite, in between, one yard forward, etc. Switch roles and let the child give you directions.

HERE'S WHAT ELSE:

Give the child a large blank sheet of paper and a crayon. Inform him that he will be making a picture by doing what you tell him to draw. Begin with simple instructions, such as, "In the middle of the paper, draw a circle." Other good directional terms are left side, right side, top/bottom, and above/below. Vary the design (circle, square, line, etc.) and the instructions as the child's skill increases. For example, "Make a square above the circle." Gradually introduce different colors and combine concepts. For example, "Draw a blue square with a red circle around it."

Treasure Hunt

HERE'S HOW: At home, before going
shopping, prepare the list of
items to be purchased (see
"Making a List, Checking It
Twice"). When you're shopping,
the child will be able to identify
items on the shelf by using the
pictures, labels, etc., on his list.
There are many levels of product identification the child can
be tested on. First, the product
itself (milk). Then, the particular
brand name of the product
(brand x). Next, the size or
amount of the product (half-
gallon). For younger children,
limit this activity to one section
of the supermarket, such as
cereal.

HERE'S WHAT ELSE: Find a stimulating picture in a children's book or magazine. Ask the child to identify "all things that are shaped like a circle." Use different sizes and colors. For example, "Can you find the smallest brown dog?" Ask older children to find "everything that is alive" or "all things that grow."

Your Order, Please

HERE'S HOW: In a restaurant, have the
child draw pictures or write the
names of the food and drinks
that are ordered. Family members may need to repeat their
order for the child to be able to
remember all the items. If time
permits, the child can make
small signs to place in front of
each person that indicate his
order.

HERE'S WHAT ELSE: At home or while waiting in
a restaurant, reminisce about
family holiday dinners. Ask the
child to recall the foods served
for Thanksgiving dinner. Special
family gatherings, such as a
Fourth of July picnic, can in-
spire the heartiest of appetites.

Sign It

HERE'S HOW:
Make a game of looking for words on printed signs that begin with each letter of the alphabet. Begin with A and continue through the alphabet. The words can be located anywhere on the sign. Words beginning with letters such as Q, X, and Z are more difficult to find. These letters may need to be eliminated from this activity.

HERE'S WHAT ELSE:
Play a letter game by using the rules of Bingo. Make a card with nine squares, each square having one letter.

The Shape of Things to Come

HERE'S HOW: Give the child a box of buttons. Encourage the child to
think of things to do with the
buttons. One idea is to separate
the buttons according to shape,
that is, into circles, squares,
ovals, and irregular shapes. Do
the same for colors. Also, make
different shapes by arranging
the buttons. For instance, round
buttons can be shaped into a
circle.

HERE'S WHAT ELSE: After the child is able to
group the buttons into various
categories, have the child select
buttons and name them by category, by saying, for example,
one red button, two round buttons, etc. Also, set up a pattern
of buttons, such as one red,
one blue, and one green. After
the child looks at this design,
have him copy your pattern.

3

THE TREND IS GROWING ~
THE REWARDS ARE SHOWING
Activities for Children Aged 7
and Older

A Special Way to Show a Special Day

HERE'S HOW: For this activity you will need a large calendar, a crayon, and a package of happy-face stickers. Explain to the child that you and he are going to identify the days during the year that bring us close together and make us happy because we are with the people who are special to us. Beginning with the current month, point out to the child the dates that are appropriate to the activity, such as birthdays and holidays. Then have the child circle the date and place a sticker on the number. This calendar can be kept to remind the child of coming events.

HERE'S WHAT ELSE: Select a day for the child to be "king" or "queen for the day." To mark this day, place a picture of the child on a certain day on the calendar. To make this day special, let your child pick the menu for dinner, watch his favorite television shows, sit in Mom's or Dad's seat at the dinner table, and choose a special activity. It is recommended that each member of the family participate to express appreciation for those people who are special to you.

Word Jumble

HERE'S HOW: Using capital letters, print the alphabet on cards (one letter per card). Select ten letters, making sure to include several vowels. Randomly place these cards on a flat surface. Show the child how to make a word from the letters. Have the child make as many words as he can from the letters. Encourage basic words, such as to, an, in, on, at. Change letters often to avoid frustration.

HERE'S WHAT ELSE: Following the same procedure, use lowercase letters and blends (bl, cl, dr, br).

What's It Made Of?

HERE'S HOW:
Using the "Category Game" procedure (see page 50), name an object or concept and break it down into its parts. For instance, if the object is a car, then appropriate responses would be wheels, seats, lights, brakes, windows, and radio. Some suggested objects and concepts are tossed salad, house, school, forest, and playground.

HERE'S WHAT ELSE:
Vary the game by naming an item, such as soup, and let the child make five guesses to figure out what ingredient in the soup you are thinking about.

Rhyme Time

HERE'S HOW: Using construction paper,
make a rhyme clown by cutting
ten circles (6 inches in diame-
ter) to be used for clown faces.
Cut ten triangles the same size,
to be used for the clowns' hats.
Have the child color and decorate all the clowns' faces and
hats—which are to remain unat-
tached. Then print a different
word on each clown's face and
a matching rhyming word on
each hat. For example, a face
with the word "run" printed on it
would match a hat with a rhyming word such as "sun" printed
on it. Mix up all the pieces. Have
the child match the rhyming
words by putting the face and
hat together.

HERE'S WHAT ELSE: Design caterpillars by making small circles for the heads and tubular strips for the bodies. Make three times as many heads as bodies. The heads will be used to complete word endings. On the body of each caterpillar, print a word ending, such as "ing," "at," "in." On the head, print letters that will make a word when the child places the correct beginning letter in front of the ending. Thus, a word will be formed when the head and body of the caterpillar are joined.

What Was I Before?

HERE'S HOW:

To play the game "What was I before?" tell the child to pretend he is ketchup in a bottle or butter on a slice of bread. Then ask the question, "What were you before you became ketchup?" Continue the game until the child is able to determine the primary source of the finished product; for example, ketchup is made from tomatoes, which grew on a vine.

HERE'S WHAT ELSE:

Try this game by starting with the basic raw ingredient, such as tomatoes. Ask the question, "I once was a tomato, and now I am . . . ?"

Road Signs for Backseat Drivers

HERE'S HOW:

Before leaving on a car trip, make copies of road signs. You can make a stop sign by cutting a hexagon out of red paper. Print words neatly on each sign and place all the signs in an envelope. Have the child match the correct road sign in his envelope with the actual road sign where it is seen along the highway. Each paper road sign can be marked on the back as being worth a certain number of points. In the city, traffic signals may be worth less because they are more common and major route signs worth more. The variance in points will make the child more aware of shifting environments. Add up points and cash them in at the next rest stop.

HERE'S WHAT ELSE:

With paper and markers, let the child win *extra* points by drawing road signs different from those in the envelope.

No Hamburger in the Salad, Please

HERE'S HOW:

This is a "hands-on" activity that can be done after returning from a shopping trip or if you have a pantry in which you have these foods. Get your child to arrange grocery items by category. (To use as a rainy day activity, have the child make a list of the items present, then, categorize them.) Suggested categories and examples of each are listed below.

Food Type: dairy, meat, vegetable, fruit.

Composition: liquid, dry (granular), solid.

Packaging: jar, paper, bottle, can, box.

Temperature Requirements: frozen, fresh, refrigerated.

Meal Times: breakfast, dinner, snack.

Person: Mom, Dad, brother, self, all.

Consumption: edible, household, decorative, special treats.

Older children can arrange
items according to:
Weight: ounce, pound, gram.
Nutritional Value: carbohydrates,
calories, vitamins.
Cost: less than $2.00, between
$2.00 and $5.00, more than
$5.00.

HERE'S WHAT ELSE:

Set up a "mini" store in
your home by giving the child
items from several categories,
such as paper products, toys, or
treats. Select an area that can
be divided into sections. Identify
each section by the category,
such as "candy counter" and
"toy section." Together with the
child, write the price of each
item on a card and fold the
card so it stands up next to the
object. Have the child place the
objects for sale in the appropriate sections. Play money and
toy cash registers can add creative fun.

Shelf a Sheet and Tally the Towels

HERE'S HOW:

This activity is great for spring cleaning, when cupboards and closets need freshening. Utilize linen closet cleaning as a learning and helping activity by preparing ahead of time two identical sets of shelf labels made from colored construction paper. Make labels for all items to be taken out of the closet; such as towels, sheets, and pillow cases. Before each item is removed, mark the shelf by taping the prepared label on the shelf edge. Put the second set of labels where the items are to be placed (on the bed or on the carpet). Have the child match the linen to the label. Replace all linen on proper shelf. For younger children, use pictures of the items for identification or place a sample item in front of each label.

HERE'S WHAT ELSE: To reorganize other items in the house, have the child sort the silverware by separating the knives, forks, and spoons; stack the pots by size; and count all the pillows in the house.

Squaring Off

HERE'S HOW:

Cut out an eight-inch square of construction paper. Then, cut the square into four pieces, each a different angle and size. Pieces should resemble triangles, rectangles, and irregular shapes. Mix up the pieces. Have the child put the pieces together again to form a square. This is a more difficult activity than it appears, since there are numerous combinations when both sides of the paper are identical. To simplify this task, make a duplicate pattern of the jigsaw puzzle so that the child can match the pieces by placing them on top of the pattern.

HERE'S WHAT ELSE:

Have the child make a picture using the shapes. Glue or paste the shapes on paper to form a picture of something known or just a geometric design.

One More Time

HERE'S HOW:

Construct a clock out of paper cups. In a circle, place twelve paper cups that have been numbered 1 through 12. Remove any two paper cups from the circle and have the child indicate which numbers are missing. Then have the child replace the cups in the appropriate position. After the child can successfully replace cups in the circle, rearrange the cups and have the child reconstruct the clock.

HERE'S WHAT ELSE: In the center of the circle, place a small cardboard circle and attach two strips of construction paper for hands. Give the child either two pennies or two beans. Have the child put one penny in the 12 o'clock cup and one penny in any other cup. Have the child turn the hands of the clock to match the cups with the pennies. Instruct the child that the cup he has selected indicates a specific time. To reinforce learning, be sure the child repeats the number selection three times. Next, you select a number (time) and have the child drop the pennies correspondingly.

Another Mile, Another Memory

HERE'S HOW:

Before going on a long trip, purchase or make a scrapbook. A scrapbook can be made by folding sheets of construction paper in half and stapling the sheets inside a folder or plastic binder. In the scrapbook could be kept postcards, pictures from tourist brochures, maps, and souvenir placemats or napkins from restaurants.

HERE'S WHAT ELSE:

So that the child can expand his mementos of the trip, add blank paper for drawing to the folder. The child can draw and color sights he sees along the way that impress him. A billboard showing an alligator or an airplane might make an interesting memento.

4

REASONING SKILLS ~
SUPPLEMENT FOR
THE SCHOOL-AGE CHILD

Reasoning skills can be taught and strengthened while your child is enjoying a "puzzle"-type activity. When prepared on three-by-five-inch cards, these activities can be stored for future use.

To achieve the best results, begin with Level 1 exercises and proceed through all steps. Once the total process is complete (Step 4), the content can be changed to introduce additional skills and higher levels of thinking (Levels 2 through 5). Each level in this program requires the child use a different reasoning process.

The thinking process needed in these reasoning skill activities has two basic steps. First, the child must "decode" or see a sequence or pattern developing. Then, the child must *think* of how to complete or continue the sequence or pattern. This is achieved by studying the Key Set, or the first set. The Key Set is a series of three blocks that have numbers, letters, or symbols in them. Together, the three numbers, letters, or symbols have a special relationship; they follow some sequence or pattern.

The first task for the child is to identify the relationships among the numbers, letters, or symbols in the Key Set. For example, all three numbers may follow in a natural counting order. Letters could follow in alphabetical order. The same procedure is used with symbols as with numbers and letters.

After the child can identify the sequence in the Key Set, the next task is to apply that sequence to another set with the same pattern as the Key Set. This second set will contain an empty block or answer space. The child will fill in the answer space based on the information given in that set and the previous Key Set. In order to understand the exercise, turn to Level 1, Step 1 Activity. Note: Key Set contains three numbers in sequence (1, 2, 3). Set 2 requires the child to complete a series of three numbers in sequence (6, 7, 8). Since the emphasis is three numbers in sequence, it is not important to the activity that numbers are missing between Key Set and Set 2.

In Step 2 a third set is added. The third set requires two answers. When Set 3 is completed, increase the activity by adding another row of blocks to each of the three sets (Step 3). This follows with a third row of blocks so that the finished set contains nine blocks (Step 4).

Follow the same procedure for Levels 2 through 5. A sample of how to expand on all levels is given in Level 1, labeled, Level 1, Expansion. In the expansion exercise, the answer spaces are placed at the beginning, middle, or end of each set, alternating with the blank spaces.

Level 1 — Step 1

KEY SET

SET 2

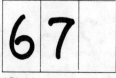

(Numbers in
sequence)

(Child completes
sequence)

(Letters in
alphabetical order)

(Child completes
sequence)

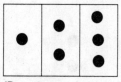

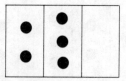

(Dots increasing
in number)

(Child makes 4-
dot pattern)

Level 1 — Step 2

KEY SET   SET 2   SET 3

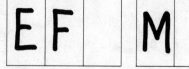

(Numbers in
sequence)

(Child completes Sets 2 and 3)

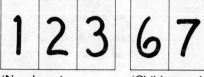

(Letters in
alphabetical order)

(Child completes Sets 2 and 3)

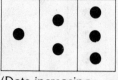

(Dots increasing
in number)

(Child completes Sets 2 and 3)

Level 1 — Step 3

KEY SET   SET 2   SET 3

1	2	3
A	B	C

6	7	
E	F	

9		
M		

(Combining a row of numbers and a row of letters. At this point different numbers and letters should be used to avoid memorization. This example uses the same letters and numbers to illustrate the format)

(Child completes Sets 2 and 3)

Level 1 — Step 4

KEY SET   SET 2   SET 3

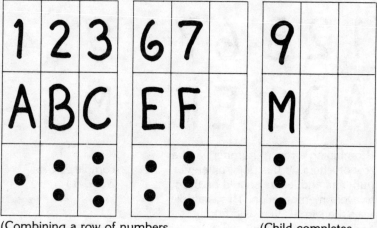

(Combining a row of numbers,   (Child completes
letters, and dots)   Sets 2 and 3)

Level 1 — Expansion

(NO KEY) SET 1   SET 2   SET 3

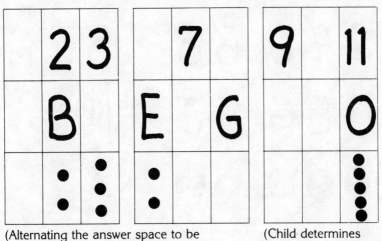

(Alternating the answer space to be at the beginning, middle, or end of each set)

(Child determines the sequence)

Level 2 — Sample

KEY SET   SET 2   SET 3

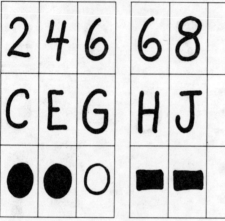 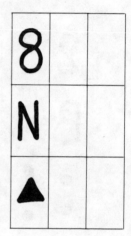

(Numbers increase by 2)

(Letters skip 1 in sequence)

(2 solid designs, followed by 1 blank design)

Level 3 — Sample

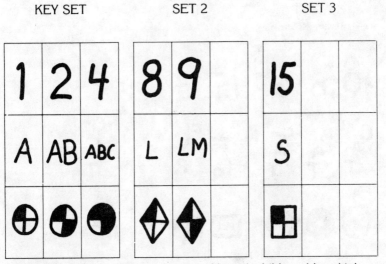

KEY SET   SET 2   SET 3

(Numbers fall two in order, skip one. Note: A child could multiply second numeral by 2)

(Letters are added on, one additional letter per block in sequence.)

(Design is shaded top-left quadrant first, then top-left and bottom-right quadrants, followed by top-left, top-right, and bottom-right quadrants)

Level 4 — Sample

KEY SET   SET 2   SET 3

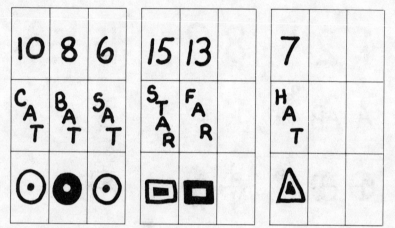

(Numbers decrease by 2)

(Words rhyme)

(Design is shaded center, then blank center, followed by shaded center)

Level 5 — Sample

KEY SET	SET 2	SET 3

 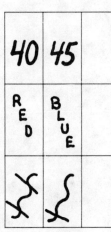

(Numbers increase by 5)

(Objects are of the same category)

(Diagonal lines and shapes disappear)

EDUCATIONAL SKILL ~ REFERENCE GUIDE

* Memory is subdivided to distinguish the ability to store and recall what one has heard (auditory memory) from what one has seen (visual memory).
† Motor skills are subdivided into gross motor skills (including posture, balance, sitting, standing, jumping, hopping, kicking, rhythm) and fine motor skills (including grasping and manipulating objects, cutting, painting, puzzles, pasting).